MW01004833

# THE EMPTY CHAIR

## the journey of grief after suicide

written by **Beryl S. Glover**
edited by **Glenda Stansbury**

# In-Sight Books

1st printing–December, 1999

Copyright©2000 by In-Sight Books, Inc.
P. O. Box 42467
Oklahoma City, Oklahoma 73123
1-800-658-9262
www.insightbooks.com

Manufactured in the United States of America

ISBN 1-892785-34-X

*Photos by Ted West Photography*

*In celebration of my daughter,*
*Catherine Elizabeth Glover*
*and in memory of her dad,*
*Robert Hoyt Glover*
*and in honor of my sons,*
*Dave and Tim Glover*

*Eternal thanks to my fellow journeymen for trusting in me and sharing their stories. Recognizing the anguish associated with reliving their experiences, I appreciate the time they have given on behalf of those who will travel this road in the future.*

*–Beryl*

*The kitchen table* is a family focal point—a center for school projects, cookie decorating, sharing the day's events over an evening meal. A place for watching TV, doing homework, making plans.

When our loved one dies, there is all too suddenly an empty chair at the table. We may rearrange the furniture, purchase a new table, or even move to another location. The fact is that life at that table has been forever altered and the hole in our hearts cannot be mended by removing or replacing the empty chair.

# A SUICIDE IN THE FAMILY...

Time stands still. For a little while or a long while. Whereas the world whispers its regrets and then continues on, our body shuts down. At first, we measure time in breaths. We can't move, we can't eat, we can't think, we can't hear, we can't sleep. We feel desperate and disconnected. Disconnected from our loved one in the middle of a sentence. Disconnected from ourselves and our lives. We are in shock, and it may last for two days, two weeks, two months...sometimes even longer.

This book describes the grief process as it is experienced by a variety of people. In it we address the emotions and expressions of grief common to most people after the death of a loved one, list them in alphabetical order, and offer stories and insights of fellow travelers. We call it the "glossary of oh-my-gods."

The people who share their stories are making progress and healing a little more each day. Their experiences are a testimonial that beyond the suffocating pain and terrible sadness, there is life and there is hope.

This book is about what happens after the initial days of the funeral. It is about what to do when we get up the next morning and everyone has gone home. Home to resume life, leaving us with the staggering task of forging a way to go from where we are—drowning—to returning to some semblance of life as we knew it.

*There is no grief which time does not lessen and soften.*

*Cicero [106-43BC]*

**The note on her door said**, "Please don't disturb. I stayed up late doing homework and don't have a class until 1:00."

We honored our daughter, Cathy's, request as she knew we would, notwithstanding the temptation to check in to see whether she was all right. She wasn't. She was dying a slow death by her own hand.

I listened for her every time I went upstairs that morning. I even noticed that my medication and vitamins were missing from the kitchen cabinet. "Curious," I thought, "I wonder who moved them."

Later in the morning, I noticed that her door was ajar and I heard moaning sounds calling me. I went in and found her rolling on the floor, ghostly white, unable to lie still. Her bed was soaked with blood, a kitchen knife was on the night stand and there were medicine bottles scattered everywhere. She begged me to open some windows because she couldn't breathe. I knew as soon as I saw her that she was dying.

Automatic pilot took over. With a composure that belied my terror, I ran downstairs and asked my sister-in-law to call my husband, Bob, the rescue squad and Cathy's surgeon. The rescue squad instructed me to hold her slashed wrists so she wouldn't lose more blood. I ran back to her room and desperately followed those instructions. I knew there was not much blood left in her body, but I was too frightened to do anything else. I was so intent on doing precisely what I was told that I didn't even take her in my arms—a memory that will always hurt.

The rescue squad was there in five minutes and a police officer shortly thereafter. The medics listened for a pulse. I informed them that I had given Cathy a kidney two years earlier. They asked some questions and then injected her with something. They then moved her onto a gurney and into the ambulance, radioed the Emergency Room and we were on our way.

Bob came home just as help arrived and followed us to the hospital. We were ushered into a small room and attended by some very gentle staff members. Cathy's surgeon stepped in and assured us that everything possible was being done and he would keep us informed. We waited and talked a little and, shortly, he returned and said simply, "I'm sorry. We did everything we could, but there was no hope of saving her."

Time stopped. I couldn't breathe. Bob began to sob and I stared at the wall, shocked into silence. Someone softly touched my arm and invited me to cry. The tears would come later. Our beloved, and only, daughter was dead. We had faced such a possibility many times before, never believing that it could happen.

Still on automatic pilot, we thanked everyone and left the hospital clutching one another. It certainly wasn't the first time we'd left Cathy in a hospital, but it would be the last. Shock relieved us of some of what would soon become indescribable pain as we contemplated the horror of what had just happened.

Driving home alone together—I have no idea how we accomplished that—we started to talk about the immediate questions of funeral directors, churches, the disposition of Cathy's body and those necessary logistics that we are compelled to address at the end of a life.

Such questions were fresh in our minds for we had lost my brother, John, three weeks earlier to suicide. Chronically depressed and suffering from severe insomnia for more than a year, he had finally taken his own life to escape the pain of yet another depression coming on.

Kevin, the funeral director who handled my brother's services, was a natural choice for us. We knew Kevin to be an unusually wise and immensely kind professional. We trusted him completely. It was an enormous relief that he could come.

Then we called Bill, our beloved minister from a church family of some twenty years past. He said the last thing he wanted to do was to conduct a memorial service for Cathy, but he would be there. Another enormous sigh of relief.

After those details were settled, I wandered out onto the patio and sank into a rocking chair. I looked up at the heavens and listened to the wind rustling through the leaves. I had to think. I felt completely alone. How could I survive this tragedy? Still numb from the shock of my brother's suicide, here I was facing my worst nightmare. The unspeakable had happened to me. My daughter of 23 years, my pal, had chosen to end her life and she had taken my kidney with her.

I didn't want to live either if living meant I was to be here and she was to be somewhere else. Forever. If I sat there long enough, maybe God would send a message that the leaves would translate into sounds my earthly ears could understand. I needed some assurance that He was waiting for her to come through the heavenly gates and join His Kingdom. In any case, I couldn't stand a roof over my head. I simply couldn't let anything interfere with my view of the sky.

I sat there for hours and hours and rocked and rocked, crying and thinking and hurting and remembering. People came and went and the phone rang continuously. My brain was racing. I had to come to terms, right then, with the haunting question—where had Cathy gone? All of a sudden, just like that, I could not see her. Had she taken her medication? Had she eaten the right food and had enough liquid that day? Was the phlebitis in her leg bothering her? All the daily details my brain had become so thoroughly conditioned to thinking about my daughter became an unbearable agony.

And, yet, my religious underpinnings whispered the reassuring lessons I had learned—that Cathy was en route to Heaven. Maybe she was, but how could I be sure? I needed to know with the same certainty that I knew where she was when I tucked her into bed all those nights of her life. As tormenting as that was, I somehow figured out in those early hours that I wouldn't know for sure for a long time. Not until it was time for me to join her. In the meantime, there wasn't a choice. I would have to trust in her faith and mine.

But how would I ever learn to put one foot in front of the other, to get back on my feet, to go on with the rest of my life? Not now, not tomorrow, not ever—I couldn't stand the pain.

**From the beginning,** I recognized the challenge, but had no earthly idea how, or whether, I could meet it. Only over time did I understand the possibilities. Although suicide was new to me, I possessed some generic skills to bring to the task. One tiny step at a time and, with the support of some extremely empathic people who would help me find my way, I could nurture myself into believing once again in my life.

That's right—I said "nurture myself." In the end, this is solitary work. It does not happen in weeks or even months. It takes a long time to learn how to integrate the suicide of your loved one into your own reality and go forth into your future.

One of my friends, Donna, says it so well: "You do it the way you are." For most of us, that means searching for help where experience tells us it is likely to be available. Just like we reach for Drano® when the sink is clogged. If it works, the problem is solved. If it doesn't, we call the plumber and he advises us of the alternatives.

Our approach to grief is a little like attending to the clogged drain. We search immediately around us at first, and if we find that our resources are insufficient, we widen our search for better alternatives.

For as many people as have recovered from this experience, there are ways to do it effectively. There is no blueprint. Each of us must adapt and create our own path. The passage by which you seek resolution of your grief will begin with techniques you have used to handle difficult situations in the past. In time, you will distinguish those techniques and then adjust them to your present circumstances. You may also generate some additional tools as you recognize the need for them.

**It is only in retrospect** that I understand the prophetic decision that our family made in the beginning. We would take our first apprehensive steps in the name of life at the same time that we began to mourn our loss. We would prepare a service to celebrate Cathy's life while we grieved her death. She was a high-spirited, charismatic gal who loved life and who lived it with considerable enthusiasm. In honoring her, we wanted to honor that.

Her dad and her brother, Dave, mustered wondrous courage and offered beautiful eulogies which reflected her spirit. The music I chose included Beethoven's effervescent work from the Ninth Symphony, the hymn "Joyful, Joyful We Adore Thee," as well as "God of Our Fathers," with the trumpets sounding. If Cathy was going to Heaven, we wanted God to know she was coming and He'd better be ready, because she was sure to wake everybody up!

The morning after her service, Bob insisted that we, her surviving family, climb Baldwin Mountain together. Our two young sons—David, a college junior, and Tim, a high school sophomore—joined us. It was an immensely powerful and sustaining symbol that our life's journey would continue together. Recognizing that Cathy's absence would forever change us, that we would eternally mourn the empty chair at our table. But her final letter, with its emphatic directive to "get on with your lives" would be honored. No matter what.

At the top of the mountain, we met up with some hang gliders. Adventurous folk jumping off the cliffs with brightly colored mechanical wings attached to their bodies, soaring into the sky. It was the perfect metaphor for our daughter's decision to forsake her mortal journey and move on to what she believed would be an eternal, Heavenly life. She would continue her journey there while awaiting our arrival.

The next day, we put Dave on an airplane to resume his college studies. I remember wondering, as we rode the escalator to the terminal, whether there is an escalator to Heaven, and envisioning the musicians standing on the stairs sounding Cathy's progress. Permanently engraved in my mind is that poignant reminder of the sense of arrival and loss that accompany the frequent visits to airports so much a part of our contemporary culture. Our Cathy was gone, departed on a stairway lined with golden trumpeters, while a winged monster took our beloved son away from us an impossible 2,000 miles back to college. He might as well have been going to Mars. It felt like tragedy upon tragedy.

The difference between their departures was all tangled up in a swelling of emotions I couldn't begin to unravel, forcing me to face the beginning of a journey I didn't want to undertake. I had no previous experience for the job and no models to emulate. I was on my own without a tool kit and I was terrified.

That was the way I felt then. But, I soon learned that I did have some critical available resources. One was a dear family friend, Loey, who had lost three of her seven children. One daughter died an infant death, one son by accidental drowning and one son by an automobile accident. None by suicide, admittedly, but I believed that she understood the enormity of the task I was facing. In the beginning she was my lifeline.

Loey sent me a card right after Cathy's death that had the following inscription: "Hurts have taught me never to give up loving. Be willing to take another risk and chance, otherwise tomorrow may be empty." It was a potent message, a profound challenge offered with boundless love, and I heard it very clearly. Indeed, it became a dominant theme of my recovery.

Loey and I talked on the phone a great deal and she gently made suggestions of ways I could nurture myself. "Feel the pain," she would say, "don't run from it. You've got to feel it fully before you can come to grips with it. Hold yourself—put your arms around yourself and hold your own hands and let the tears come. Feel the comfort of being gentle with yourself, of allowing yourself to express your pain as often as you need to." I did, and it helped… a lot.

Mostly I learned that Loey's instincts were right for me. My grief work would have to begin right away. I had to acknowledge it, live with it, examine it, allow it to take whatever form it would before I could begin to heal. I had to crawl again before I could walk. I learned to go to bed, curl into a fetal position and cry until there were no more tears. I discovered that there was temporary relief in my crying, and then the tears would begin to accumulate again and the cycle would repeat itself. Almost imperceptibly I learned that, in time, my tears accumulated more slowly and in diminishing quantity.

During those early days there were times when I didn't think I would ever feel like living again, when tears flowed into rivers wherever I happened to be. Tears that I couldn't and didn't hold back. Anything and everything reminded me of Cathy. I looked for her and saw her everywhere. I cried in the grocery store when I saw food that she loved. I cried when I walked along the street or drove my car. For the first few months, I cried nearly every time I stopped for a traffic light, sometimes so blinded by tears that I had to pull off the road.

There were days, at first a great many, when I couldn't bear to face the future without Cathy. I missed her so that I would have given anything to see her again…to hold her in my arms one more time and know that she was safe…to tell her how much I love her…to say good-bye.

I took great comfort in Bill, the minister who conducted the memorial service, and his brilliant description that he shared over coffee the morning of Cathy's service. "Heaven is a soft place with bright light and lots of flowers.

Where all God's children got shoes." He paused a long time and then added, "And kidneys."

But, in the beginning, the intangible notion of all that drove me nearly to the edge myself. Without question, in those early weeks after her death, I would have given suicide serious consideration were it not for my family and for her injunction to us to get on with our lives. It was more than a passing thought on several occasions, but it was never a serious option.

The other critical resource available to me was the minister/psychologist who assisted in Cathy's service. He encouraged me to call if I needed him. I needed him all right, immediately afterward. When the pain threatened my sanity I called Neil and he would, by some miracle, arrange to see me right away. His sensitivity to my anguish was extraordinary. I had another ally, a skilled counselor, for the awesome journey that was mine.

At first we talked about Cathy. We talked about our rented house in Connecticut and her presence in, and sudden departure from, that house. We reminisced about our marvelous home in the woods in Chapel Hill where we had lived for most of her life. We talked about our life there, and about the handsome stable her dad had constructed for Candlelight, Brandy, Beauty and, especially her beloved Gypaaron, the horses who occupied her stable over the years.

We also talked about Cathy's health, beginning with bladder surgery when she was an infant, repeated during her teenage years and, finally, her kidney transplant at age 21.

We discussed the lengthy rambling letter she left us at the time of her death. It described her frustration over the ongoing limitations of her compromised health, and reflected her growing melancholy brought on by those constraints as well as the complicated drug therapy she was undergoing as a kidney transplant patient.

Neil listened raptly while I talked about Cathy and struggled to understand her death—things I needed desperately to do. And he honored my pain. He, too, encouraged me to let it out, to examine it, feel its full force. We talked about suicide and, together, we made the decision to temporarily set my brother's death aside and focus on the overwhelming immediacy of Cathy's death. We talked about what life would be like without my daughter, and we talked about healing. He encouraged me to feel my loss and, at the same time, give myself permission to honor Cathy's life and memory, to honor my family, to live again. Yes, even to laugh again.

Neil did something else for us, something that made the difference between healthy grief and a family in conflict. He invited us to take the Myers-Briggs test, a tool that identifies individual personality characteristics. The results revealed what he clearly suspected—that my husband and two sons are "intellectually" directed while I am more "feeling oriented."

It was that awareness that empowered us to honor the differences in our grief processes, to understand that no two people grieve alike. There are no universal rules.

Healthy grief takes many forms, many speeds, manifests itself in infinite ways.

The gift of helping us honor our differing methods was perhaps the most important thing that happened to our family in the course of our journey. We learned that it was okay for me to cry, for Bob to think, for our sons to get on with their young lives. Each of us would do all of those things eventually, perhaps privately, perhaps together, but the emphasis would vary greatly from one to another and at one time or another. Just as no two people experience life in the same way, we had to understand that no two people, not even family members, endure grief in the same way.

**In the beginning** we are propelled into action by a friend, the doctor, a police officer, a clergy person or a telephone call. There are a great many things to be done, decisions to be made, rituals to be performed.

Death, by any cause, initiates the important ritual of gathering to remember the deceased. It provides a structure for the days to follow. It sets us in motion, albeit robotic motion. It creates a sense of purpose.

The funeral affords us all—family, friends, associates, acquaintances—the necessary opportunity to remember and honor our loved one. To pay our respects, to offer our love and condolences, to view the body, to say a collective good-bye, to bring bread and break it together, to remember and exchange stories, to comfort one another, to preserve the bonds.

page 22 

So it is that we are launched into the death event with its relative idiosyncrasies and customs which are all accomplished with as much dignity as possible. This event has a beginning and an ending. But, it is merely the introduction to the journey.

Next comes the main event, the hard work of mourning, when the shock begins to wane and the reality of our loss gradually emerges. The main event is when our pain sets in in earnest. Some of us look our grief directly in the face. Others protect ourselves until we know we can bear it. We peek at it every now and then, and open the window wide only when we have gathered what we hope are the critical resources to withstand it. No matter how long it takes, knowing when we are ready to face our grief full force is an essential element.

My guess is if we had any idea of the enormity of the challenges ahead of us on that fateful morning after, some of us might give up then and there. It will be a long time before we recognize that we simply never will return to "normal," if normal is who we were before tragedy befell us.

The task is to superimpose the suicide of our loved one—spouse, child, sibling, parent, lover, ex-lover, friend—onto our own life tapestry. To come to terms with it so that the energy invested initially in survival may gradually be directed toward the quality of our future.

**All of us** who experience this loss differ in many ways. Some of us become ill; some become embittered, embattled, hostile, or angry; some withdraw; some become more sensitive, loving and appreciative of life. Some of us may experience many of these feelings at different times during our grief work.

Some of us know why our loved one completed suicide—some do not. Some are dealing with multiple suicides, or a suicide preceded or followed directly by one or more profound losses. Some can understand, and even condone, our loved one's decision. Others believe that the suicide was senseless and the wasted life an outrage.

One thing is certain—we do change. The direction that change takes is ours to determine.

Some of the stories on these pages may be more relevant to your circumstances than others, but anguish, anger, desperation and hopelessness are essentially universal. Most of us experience that dark emptiness of life in the early weeks, and the painstaking work of repairing our wounded spirits.

This book is our testimonial that, beyond the suffocating pain and the terrible sadness, there is life. It is a book of hope. It is about learning how to live again by addressing your grief, doing your mourning, feeling your soul-wrenching sorrow.

Whether the death occurred last week, last year, or twenty years ago, it is never too late to address your grief. Sooner is usually better than later, but later is better than not at all.

Take heart in knowing that Spring comes after the leaves have fallen and the earth has slept. There is new life in each of us, creatures of the earth, after our spirits have wilted and died. It may not have the same luster, but it is surely worthwhile. Your empty chair will someday represent the goodness of the life that is departed.

*Like the dance of brilliant reflections on a clear pond, well-being is a shimmer that accumulates from many important life choices made over the years by a mind that is not often muddied by pretense or ignorance and a heart that is open enough to sense people in their depths and to intuit the meaning of most situations. . .Well-being registers deep in our unconscious. It is an accumulated attitude, a sustained background tone of equanimity behind the more intense contrasts of daily events, behind even periods of unhappiness.*

Gail Sheehy, *Pathfinders*

***Acceptance***—Accepting the reality of our loved one's suicide is the centerpiece of our recovery. It is a zigzag course that begins somewhere in the early weeks of our journey. There are moments when we can see beyond the tangle of our shrieking emotions and begin to acknowledge our loss. There are other times when it's just too horrible to countenance, and we deny it hopelessly.

This zigzag course is just that. It eventually takes us in the right direction—forward rather than backward. However, our progress is routinely interrupted by setbacks. After months, sometimes even longer, of what may seem a never-ending struggle along this difficult continuum, we eventually learn to acquiesce to the suicide as part of our new reality.

### *Elizabeth*

Elizabeth is a physician. She is married to a physician and the mother of four young adults. Her mother completed suicide over thirteen years ago at age 70.

Elizabeth remembers the moment:

*She hanged herself. I mean, time stands still. I remember I was in the kitchen. Our kids were involved in skating lessons, and I had just come from a lesson when the police called. They had gone to my mother's house and found her. I'm not sure whether they said she had killed herself, but I understood that was what they thought had happened. And I was absolutely dumbstruck.*

> *My mother really hadn't a clue as to what the impact on her family would be, nor how important she was to us. I think she thought that Ben and I had the children and that she was not as essential to me as she had once been. She would probably be amazed that thirteen years later, I would spend hours in someone's den discussing her death.*

Elizabeth expects to feel a part of the grief for the rest of her life, but she acknowledges a shift in its intensity with the passing of time.

> *You wake up and you have this great deep sadness, and you're swimming around in it like a noodle in soup. The turning point is when you wake up in the morning and feel sort of happy. You don't think 'Oh my God.' You wake up and say, 'Gee, it's a lovely day.' Maybe the grieving process begins to end when corn-on-the-cob tastes good again!*

Acceptance is an all-important threshold in our grief work. Take heart when you sense that it is within reach, for it is a most encouraging signpost.

*Anger*—Feeling anger toward a person who has chosen death is a normal reaction to what, in many but not all circumstances, was a poor decision and it merits our full attention.

One woman describes her anger:

> *For years I've been dealing with anger*
> *toward my mother for leaving my sisters and me*
> *and not sharing in our accomplishments. One way*
> *I've struggled through that is in my job. I'm*
> *constantly trying to be the best. My dad remarried*
> *and we had a reasonably well-adjusted family life.*
> *But, I still ache for this biological mother who*
> *gave birth to me and who was with me for most of*
> *my younger years.*

There are many manifestations of anger:

We may feel anger toward our family members
   whose grief is expressed differently from
   our own.
We may feel angry with our loved one's medical
   caregivers.
We may be angry at a friend who said something
   inappropriate.
We may feel anger toward a survivor who falls
   short of our expectations and who
   heightens our sense of deprivation.
We may feel anger toward someone to whom
   the victim confided suicidal thoughts and
   who honored that trust.
We may be angry with God.


My own anger was multifaceted, and it took years to
differentiate it. I was angry with my brother for making
what I believed was a poor decision—for ending his

interesting and talented life. I was angry that he left behind a wife and two young children. I was angry at the heartache he imposed on all of us. I was angry that his decision evidently legitimized suicide for Cathy. And, of course, I was angry with Cathy for giving in to her despair and ending her young life.

During the first year or two, as I struggled to understand the enormity of it all, I had some healthy temper tantrums. Alone in the house, I would crawl into bed and wail my heart out. I discovered that it was a harmless and surprisingly effective way to release the anger that accumulated within. Those episodes occurred quite regularly at first, and I would feel better for some time afterward. Then, the cycle would begin again.

People find some interesting physical outlets for their anger. One woman buys all the dishes she can find at garage sales. Then, when she is consumed by anger, she will take the dishes and break them into the dumpster.

Several families in a small Texas town who lost teenagers in tragic car accidents, have an unusual tradition. They bring hard boiled Easter eggs to the driving range and blast them with their golf clubs.

In searching for a pressure valve for anger, whatever works, without creating harm to yourself or others, is okay.

What eventually relieved my anger was an evolving understanding of both of the suicides. It was a hard-fought accomplishment. What I understood I could learn to accept, even though I could not condone their decisions.

Anger knows no boundaries. It is often disabling and it doesn't normally disperse voluntarily. It is advisable to take heed of it and give your best effort to its resolution.

## *Anniversaries*—Anniversaries are the special days we associate with our loved one such as the date of the death, the birthday, holidays or special events that traditionally included the person. They are rarely forgotten and they push our emotional buttons in ways that magnify our awareness of the loss we have sustained.

For me, Cathy's birthday continues to be especially difficult for two reasons. The first is that I think mothers typically bring a unique vulnerability to a child's birth date because of the myriad remembrances of pregnancy, delivery, infant care, etc. I tend to re-live it every year, which inevitably reminds me of her death and usually brings on a certain melancholy.

The second reason is that it is on May 14th, which always falls around Mother's Day. Two years after her death, we left on that day for Texas for Dave's graduation and wedding. My excitement was temporarily confused with an intensified awareness of her loss. I also was aware of the sadness of knowing how much she would have enjoyed being with us, how much merriment she would have brought to those events and, of course, how much she would be missed.

Another year, her birthday fell on the day before Mother's Day and we were in Phoenix. We gave that a great deal of thought because there is an Arabian horse farm in nearby Scottsdale which Cathy had always dreamed of visiting. Not knowing when we might be in Phoenix again, Bob and I decided that it was fitting that we visit the farm on that day. The decision was complicated because the subject of horses was an especially painful one I had studiously protected myself from. Some five years after Cathy's death, here was a chance to address it and I sensed it was time.

We invited an old friend to join us and had a good time driving around the farm, looking at the barns, paddocks, brood mares and babies and reminiscing rather gaily about life with Cathy and her beloved Arabian gelding, Gypaaron. It turned out that, while it required careful planning and preparation, it was a wise decision.

It was inevitable that one year it would fall on Mother's Day. That year we were in Baltimore and chose to spend it doing something we were certain would be soothing. We went to the famous Baltimore Aquarium and had an engaging and relaxing morning. It felt right. We have learned much about how to take care of ourselves on that day.

The anniversary of Cathy's death, September 19th, is another tough day. I often buy a plant, a pleasing symbol of life, on that anniversary as well as on her birthday. For years, we went out to dinner that evening on the premise that we wanted to pause together and remember. And, it helped us to weather it more effectively to have something to look forward to at day's end.

Anniversaries are an eternal part of life after our loved one's death. Be prepared. They are exceptionally difficult during the first year's cycle. But the intensity of the pain can gradually yield to more poignant remembrances and eventually to enjoying happy memories.

**Blame**—Blame involves a number of dimensions. We may blame the suicide victim for making a poor decision. We may blame ourselves for overlooking something that might have contributed to it. We may blame another person for any number of reasons.

We may have had an untimely argument with our loved one, or not been as understanding as we should have been, or not recognized some signals that appear in retrospect to have been clear messages. We may not have been as available as we could have been, or as loving during that last phone call and on and on.

In the end, we are faced with the simple fact of the matter. The decision our loved one made was his or her decision. It was not ours. If we had had a vote, in most cases, we would have encouraged the person to find another solution—anything but the terrible finality of ending a life.

For those of us who condone the decision, blame is not the issue. For those who do not, we will do ourselves a profound kindness to remember that we didn't make it and we're not responsible for it.

## *Sarah*

Sarah's daughter, Michelle, was 26 when she hanged herself. Sarah, mother of six adult children, had lost her husband, Arthur, just two years earlier so she was no stranger to personal suffering or to the challenges that lay ahead.

Michelle had been diagnosed manic depressive three years earlier and put on substantial medication. At the time of her death she was working in another city and returned home briefly for a medical consultation.

There are remnant "if onlys" for Sarah eight years later.

*If I had been more aware of the side effects (of her medications), how to help this kid, it would have been so much easier. She was frightened by the medication, yet, because she was 26, her doctors wouldn't tell us anything.*

*I had to come to the realization that I was not responsible for Michelle's death. I hadn't caused it. There's no point in feeling guilty about something that someone else has done.*

It is likewise not appropriate to attach blame either to an individual or to the family of the suicide victim. Blame, frankly, has no place in our recovery.

*Communication*–There is an important principle regarding communication during the bereavement period. **No two people will grieve in the same way**. Whatever the relationship, we must give one another the respect and opportunity to grieve in the manner each of us chooses. Sharing suggestions sensitively is one thing—offering prescriptions is another. "You should" has no place here. "You may want to consider" has significant potential.

### Tom and Margaret

Tom and Margaret lost their 44 year-old son, Scott, who completed suicide by jumping in front of a subway. Scott had a history of manic depression and was barely holding on to a job and a personal life.

Tom brought his well-honed engineering mind to his grief. He was analytical, disciplined, objective.

He says: *I don't worry about putting the sad things out of my mind. Scott was a great guy…Life's too short to try to understand it. But the sadness is that he's gone and it's always going to be sad. It's no sadder now than it was then, and it's no sadder now than it's going to be ten years from now. Time maybe makes it easier because your memory bank has other things in it…So, when I went back to work, I was the same as the day I left as far as the workplace was concerned. Nearly everyone said 'I'm sorry about your loss.' At first I wondered what to say, so I just said, 'Thank you.' You really don't have anything to say but thank you.*

Margaret used such terms as vulnerable, childish, and unreasonable to describe some of her emotions. She dealt primarily on the level of feelings. She cried a lot and her rhythm was entirely different than Tom's.

Margaret's words: *It makes us raw and exposed. And you get very unreasonable. No one can do the right thing. If they say something, that's wrong. If they don't say anything, they don't care. You know, we get very childish. You see someone across the room and they don't speak to you so they don't like you anymore. The poor person probably didn't even see you. But you survive by going along the best you can and taking the bumps...*

*It's like being on a teeter totter. When you're feeling down, you don't want to lean on your mate and make him sad unless you can't help it. But, if you're down and your mate is up, you feel like he doesn't care. You're torn every which way. And, you know it, but it doesn't make any difference in how you feel.*

Says Tom, *When Margaret would cry— it didn't bother me. It was just not an issue. I'd just hold her. I'd comfort her and I'd feel like that was my role. And, it seemed like she cried just about right. To each his own, I guess. And, we respect each other's views and feelings.*

Tom and Margaret have lived together for nearly 50 years, surely a useful prerequisite for their success. They claim some tension as they evolved their separate styles, for the most part they manifested generosity and patience in offering mutual respect.

Bob and I nearly crossed the line. About two months into our grief he was beginning to wonder why I cried so much and I was beginning to wonder why he didn't cry very much. We took the Myers-Briggs test, and it was a stunning revelation that led to a graceful resolution. It underscored the validity of our individual differences and, with that information, our therapist guided us as we learned to affectionately respect one another.

As my friend Donna put it, "Hands off! If we don't allow one another to grieve the way we want to, then we'll screw it up. To judge the way someone else grieves is a cruel thing to do."

## Children

Another dimension of communication is disclosure to the children concerned. There are many variables to consider, in particular, their age and the nature of their relationship to the victim.

Generally, it is advisable to tell children the truth about a suicide. They really need to know what happened and we need to find a way to tell them. Maybe not all at once, but we need to work toward letting them know the truth. Otherwise, there evolves a difference between the "words and the music" and when children feel that difference, they become confused and scared. It's important that the words and the music go together.

## Public

As to disclosure outside the family, a good solution is to put "died unexpectedly" in the newspaper and circulate the truth through your network of friends. And to tell the truth if asked directly. One lie begets another, compounded by many people doing the asking and many people doing the telling. The simple truth is the healthier course in the long term.

One final thought...A friend gave me a journal after Cathy's death, and it has been a lifeline. When I am in real pain, I take pen in hand and pour my heart out into that little book. In my experience, there is remarkable comfort and relief in getting the anguish out of my stomach, as well as in knowing where it is recorded in case I need to refer to it in the future.

*Comparisons*—One of the lessons I have learned from this experience is that no two death events are alike.

My brother's suicide was a terrible shock. A very difficult job transition had apparently triggered depression and insomnia. Treatment had included hospitalization, therapy and medication. He had terminated treatment two months earlier, and was seemingly making headway until another episode of depression began. Apparently unable to face it yet again, he completed suicide.

When Cathy died three weeks later, Johnny's death was superseded, temporarily I thought. I was wrong. It was years before I could look at what his death meant to me. My grief for my child was more compelling in the beginning and I was a bit fearful of my feelings about my brother. I knew there was some anger involved, and I instinctively understood that, in time, I would figure out how to deal with it. I am at a loss as to precisely how it evolved, but I do know that, over the years and at my leisure, little by little, I became comfortable in processing my grief for my brother.

When my mom died at age 80, there was a peaceful and mystical quality to it. Her health was deteriorating and, when I called one evening, she was confused. After several failed attempts to chat with her, I hung up and called the nurse's station to check on her status. I called her a short while later, we had a good conversation, and we said our usual good-byes.

After that, I slumped onto the sofa and, for the first time, prayed that she would pass on. When the phone rang an hour later, it was the nursing home informing me that Mom had slipped away during her evening bath in the arms of her caregivers.

My husband, Bob's, premature death three years later was exactly the opposite. He succumbed to the Epstein-Barr virus which rampaged through his system in two weeks. It was an unrelenting nightmare to watch the virus destroy his body and mind.

Afterward, despite the intensity of my grief, I knew what to do. Mostly I knew from experience that I wasn't going crazy. I was just grieving for my beloved mate. I knew how to handle the practical necessities that needed my attention at the same time that I yielded to those endless months of tears that I must discharge before I can begin to heal.

Consider the story of Donna. Her life experiences have challenged her to endure the seemingly unendurable— the suicides of two loved ones, her husband and her father, followed by the tragic lingering death of her son, whom she ultimately suspected may have intended to end his life as well.

### *Donna*

Donna and her husband, Bryant, were married during World War II. Upon discharge from the service, he secured a job as a reporter on a small newspaper in a rural Massachusetts town.

Donna remembers, *He did an awfully good job. He had a beat that he covered so he knew what was going on in town all the time.*

Not seeing a future for himself at the newspaper, Bryant tried to re-enlist in the Air Force but was not qualified. He then took a factory job nearby.

As Donna says, *It was just a change and he was trying to start again somewhere. But, he wasn't in that job for more than two months when he stuck his head in the oven.*

His suicide came as a complete shock to Donna.

*I had no idea he was feeling like that. He was drinking quite a bit, but he had when he was a reporter, too.*

It was 1951, their two young sons, Nathan and Andrew were aged four months and two-and-a-half years. Donna was terrified. She had no idea how she was going to make it financially.

Donna quickly found work and then went to college to obtain her teaching degree.

Applying the wisdom of hindsight, Donna wishes she had expressed her grief after Bryant's death. But, the survival of her fledgling family had been severely undermined and responsibility for her two sons propelled her into action. She didn't have the luxury of time to grieve. Also, that was the early 1950's.

*Nobody was given time to grieve in those days. I must have grieved some, but I have no memory of it. The financial issues were discussed, but the emotional needs of the survivor were not recognized. It just wasn't mentioned, at all.*

Donna lost her father to suicide in 1965, two years after she and her sons had moved to New Hampshire, fourteen years after her husband's death and shortly after her mother's death.

*He was in a rest home because he could no longer care for himself. He cut his throat.*

Although she was not aware of any delayed reaction to Bryant's death brought about when her father died, not surprisingly, Donna did feel some guilt.

*I'd taken off for New Hampshire instead of staying home and taking care of my dad. But, I realized that his death didn't affect me nearly as much as my husband's death.*

Donna's oldest son, Andrew, was a National Merit Finalist. He received a scholarship to a prestigious school for fine arts and during the summers he worked on the coast of Maine doing set designs for summer theater.

Donna remembers, *He loved drama, loved the theater. So, he set off as soon as he graduated.*

Andrew supported himself painting, doing newspaper work, designing t-shirts and other jobs.

*He thought about leaving, but he never got around to it. He drank too much and he knew it. I learned from his notes that he had been using some drugs, although nobody talked about that.*

*Heavy drinking and fast driving are suicidal behaviors, but it took awhile for me to suspect it. I knew he was under the influence although I didn't know the details. But, I'll never know whether he meant to go off the road or whether he just did.*

Andrew had an automobile accident late at night at the age of 35. He hit a culvert, smashed the side of his head on the struts in the windshield and landed in a ditch.

*He never recovered. Never said another word. Never swallowed, never moved. He could cough. That was about it. He couldn't move anything and was probably blind.*

After two-and-a-half years in various rehab hospitals and never regaining consciousness, Andrew died at the age of 38.

To Donna, the three deaths—her husband, her father and her son—bore virtually no rela-

tionship to one another. Facing Andrew's illness
and death felt almost as though she had never
grieved before.

> *Oh, I really don't think the others made
> any difference at all. I don't know whether
> I'm any great survivor. The other two deaths
> were...well, they weren't minor, of course,
> but they didn't affect me the same way this
> one did. They were all different, completely
> different.*

Every relationship is unique. Every death event is
unique. Each inflicts distinctive suffering on our lives.
There is considerable value added in understanding the
differences as they happen to us and as they affect us.
Offering similar respect for others' experiences is equally
sensible.

## *Counseling*–Counseling can be an extremely useful
aid to our recovery.

> We need to talk about the death of our loved one
> > and a therapist is often better equipped to
> > listen than a family member or friend.
>
> We need support and validation.
>
> We need to develop a frame of reference about
> > what constitutes healthy mourning.
>
> We need to process our anger and guilt, to
> > understand our feelings.

The safety of the therapeutic environment is an ideal
climate for doing grief work. If you decide to seek it, get

recommendations from physicians, clergy or friends. If there is a therapist in your community whose known specialty is grief—that is often a very good place to begin.

Remember that chemistry is a key ingredient in a successful therapeutic relationship. If you don't feel the right connection between you and your chosen counselor, look for another.

### Barbara

Barbara is a church organist and choir director. She had divorced several years ago and moved from the large family farmhouse into an apartment in a nearby town.

The news that arrested her life came early one Sunday afternoon after church. She received a phone call from one of her former neighbors asking her to stay at home, that her close friend, Louise, was on her way over. Louise arrived shortly and told Barbara that her son, Gary, a 24- year-old troubled youth and diagnosed schizophrenic, had bought a gun and shot himself.

*I just went blank. I couldn't comprehend it, couldn't find words. I went in and sat on the couch. I just sat there, totally uncomprehending. And I hyperventilated. I went for a walk and couldn't seem either to catch my breath or get rid of my breath.*

The loss that Barbara experienced was not simply that of her son. It was a compounded, quadruple loss. Within a matter of months she had lost her husband, her home, her roots and her son.

Barbara's means of self-protection was creative and effective.

*The pain would come on in a gush, and I would be completely overcome. But it would be short-lived. I can see it clearly. It was a little window into the pain that I would peek through and then retreat immediately. This is what I did, good, bad or indifferent. And it wasn't until I began counseling that I had the courage to stand at the window without flinching and without looking away, and then, finally, I could begin to get a perspective on the whole thing.*

Six months after Gary's death, and bolstered by the security of a new job, new living circumstances and her beloved dog, Barbara had amassed the necessary courage to open that window to her pain which she had so carefully guarded. She began by seeking professional counseling. She chose as her psychotherapist a woman who had herself lost a child. Together they wholeheartedly plunged in.

*I went through an awful lot of histrionics in those counseling sessions. A good therapist stays with you and listens carefully, and holds fast. A good therapist lets you go through it, and doesn't try to stop you from going through it. She/he might offer a Kleenex®, but that's about as far as it goes.*

Barbara's therapist held her hand in loving support while she began her grief work. Work that one person cannot do for another.

*And that's when I finally began to truly experience my pain. You know, the time you realize you're going to be okay may be less important than the date of other crossroads in your grief. In my case, it was when I found the courage to stand at that window and look and not turn away.*

One important issue related to counseling is to keep a watchful eye on surviving family members and close friends. The suicide experience so dramatically upsets the equilibrium of all who are involved that someone may manifest behavior changes that warrant therapeutic attention. Take negative signals or a suicide threat seriously. It may mean some indulgence, but we have little to lose by taking someone at their word, no matter how many times they may say it.

## *Denial*–Denial is a largely automatic, self-protective stage in the grieving process. It can be an important defense against the terrible truth. It gives us time to accustom ourselves to the facts.

### *Lois*

Lois is one of seven siblings in a large Catholic family and the mother of five adult children. Lois' brother, Rob, completed suicide at age 46. He was the youngest of the siblings.

Rob was on a weekend pass from the VA Hospital, where he was being treated for alcoholism. He was staying with Lois' sister, Paddy.

*Things were looking good. He was
attending AA meetings and had lived with
Paddy for several months prior to checking
himself back in the hospital after a few
drinking episodes. When he got squared
away again, he had weekend leaves and he
was looking for work. So, we all had a lot
of hope.*

Lois feels his first attempt some months
earlier, known only to their sister, Theresa,
resulted from discouragement about his drinking.
Theresa believed that he was losing his battle
with alcoholism and he knew it.

His second attempt was successful. While
doing some carpentry work for Paddy's neighbor
one Saturday in November, Rob left to get a pack
of cigarettes. When he didn't return by evening,
the family began looking for him. The next day
Paddy called the police while they continued to
search the area. The police found him on Sunday
evening at approximately the time he would have
been checking back into the hospital. He had
hung himself in the nearby woods.

When Paddy was notified by the police, she
called Lois.

*My first reaction was like everyone
else's. I screamed, 'No, no, no.' I just didn't
think it was possible.*

She had great difficulty comprehending
Rob's death because it was so inconceivable to
her.

*You know, the disbelief that it had
happened and my first feelings of denial
were the hardest things. And, the scariness*

> *of it. We think we're not capable of certain things and then we find out that our brother was capable of committing suicide. It took a long time to come to grips with it. A long, long time.*

Denial should not be worrisome provided its presence is short-lived. It if doesn't yield within a few weeks to the reality before you, think seriously about talking it out with someone whose guidance you trust.

## *Depression*—Death is the end of hope and depression is an inevitable by-product. We turn our feelings inward—we shut down.

Our bodies reflect our feelings. We are physically and emotionally depleted. We may lose our appetite, our concentration, our interest in life. One man said, "I was so exhausted all the time that I would come home from work and go to bed. And, I stopped talking to my friends and family."

Another said, "I actually had a physical feeling in my heart, like a pressure, like it had sunk so deep it made a hole in my heart."

Barbara tells us,

> *One afternoon about a year ago, I went shopping for a book. All of a sudden, I didn't feel like going on with living. And yet, I needed this book for my business. So, I went through the*

*motions. I went home and did the next thing—*
*preparing dinner, walking the dog—I don't*
*remember what. I simply carried my depression*
*with me and went right ahead doing what I was*
*going to do.*

Temporary depression is normal, but we need not
endure it endlessly. Releasing tears is one good outlet. It
eases the physical and emotional tension that accumulates
in our body.

Other useful things include physical activity, eating and
sleeping properly, social stimulation, counseling, reading
and support groups.

It helps a great deal to maintain yourself in as healthy
a manner as possible. Pay attention to your body and your
emotions and, if depression persists, don't hesitate to seek
assistance to manage it more effectively.

***Forgiveness***—Sooner or later, it is important to forgive the suicide victim. One man's experience is classic.
His father committed suicide when he was 15 years old. He
didn't talk about it for ten years, and then he spent fifty
years feeling negatively toward him.

Finally, he began to consider it more objectively.

*I started thinking of all the fine things I knew*
*about him, his energy, his skill, his intelligence, and*
*I slowly realized that he must have suffered terri-*
*bly. Then, there came over me a sense of loving*

> *contemplation, sorrow and sympathy that dis-*
> *solved the negative feelings that had haunted me.*
> *It was healing to recognize that he had suffered so*
> *and that he needed my sympathy, not all that*
> *anger. It somehow washed away my burden.*

In order to forgive our loved one, it helps to remind ourselves that their suicide is about them. It is about *their* decision to step permanently out of their pain. It is not about the pain they left behind that they surely did not anticipate.

Another dimension of forgiveness concerns any short-comings of the people and circumstances of the suicide. A family with a suicide victim is not automatically defined as an unhealthy family. It is a family with a member who chose to end his life.

Most important is forgiving ourselves. Tom shares his insights:

> *What I've learned is this. Don't carry a guilt*
> *burden, even if there's some reason to. Forgive-*
> *ness of yourself, it's important to say. Who knows*
> *if there was something you didn't do that you*
> *should have, or you did something you shouldn't*
> *have. You don't have to figure out exactly what*
> *happened to forgive yourself.*
>
> *I forgive myself even if I did the wrong thing.*
> *If I were brooding about that all the time, I'd make*
> *myself sick and certainly useless.*

*Scott did what he wanted to do. I've got a few more years and life is short, so I think I'm doing something good in trying to help others. But, if you're gonna crawl in a corner and feel guilty the rest of your life, you're not going to do any good for yourself or anybody else. And you'll never know anyway. So, that's how I look at it.*

Forgiveness is a principal dimension of acceptance and recovery. It will substantially assist us in putting to rest our burdens about our loved one's suicide.

*Friends*—Friends are vital to our grief experience. It can be extraordinarily comforting to know they are standing by to do whatever we ask of them. In addition to their strength and loyalty, they provide the warmth of their love, their tears (yes, crying with us helps a lot) and their ability to listen to our pain and talk about our loved one.

One of the greatest blessings of my life is my friends. They have honored my grief, been available whenever I needed them, nourished and supported me while I did the hard work I had to do, and welcomed me at all times. Friends can offer no more precious gifts than those.

Friends are often, on the other hand, a surprisingly problematic ingredient. Those who have not experienced death sometimes have a difficult time knowing what to say and do, even more so in the case of a suicide death. We may struggle to deal with friends or even extended family who, with good intentions, say things that are not well advised and that may even be detrimental to our recovery.

Friends may avoid us. One woman says, "I know my friends are thinking that if they talk about it or even look at it, it may touch their lives. They're frightened of it."

Friends may not raise the subject so that we won't think about it. The truth is, of course, we never stop thinking about it, and we need to talk about it until we don't need to talk about it anymore for whatever period of time that turns out to be. Our pain is diminished a little bit each time we share it with people who care about us.

Friends may be angry. Margaret described a case in point. "One friend told me that, though she didn't know Scott, she was so angry at him that she couldn't be of any help to me until she got over that."

Our son, Dave, grew weary of friends' suggestions that they knew how he felt. He appreciated their good intentions while recognizing the impossibility of that because his experience of life with Cathy was distinctively his own. Such a statement may unintentionally serve as a discount of the uniqueness of our grief.

One difficult aspect that often occurs is the timetable friends attach to your recovery. They may offer directives, such as, "It's been a month, you really should be getting over it now." or, "I know you must still be feeling badly, but you've got to stop thinking about it."

Other unwise comments may include, "God had his reasons," or "God chooses the strongest among us to bear such pain," or even, "I think you should see a psychiatrist."

Whatever the reaction of friends may be, by definition they are usually well-intentioned. Sometimes it helps to model what we need. I learned that it was acceptable to raise the subject if I needed to talk about Cathy. I hope I was gracious in the process, but on those occasions when I wanted to bring her into a conversation, I did so.

Eventually we learn that our friends show their love in a great many ways. I was conditioned to look for bouquets of flowers as *the only* expression of love. I finally realized it was merely one—there were a great many others, all special and meaningful.

Friends who say, "You seem to be doing so well," are eager for us to return to normal. A discreet response may be, "Thanks for your encouragement, but I know I've just begun." In the case of the friend who stays away, we might call and make a lunch date. Lunch doesn't have to be a bowl of tears; it can include some discussion of our loss without taking up more than our share of the mealtime.

One close friend of mine volunteered a lengthy story about another suicide and his inability to relate to the survivor involved. Believing this to be a reflection of his discomfort, I dropped the subject. On another occasion I suggested that, at some point, I really wanted to talk with him about Cathy. Clearly unable to listen to my pain, he offered his own list of what he thought I was feeling, and then, believing the matter settled, changed the subject. We surely are easier to be with if our friends can avoid hearing or seeing our expressions of grief.

Another friend did not contact us until six years later. She said, "I've thought of you both many times. I surely lack adequate language when life seems to overwhelm." It may not be a satisfactory explanation but, again, there was no ill will involved.

One thing to remember is that friends cannot read our minds. Barbara's advice may be universally appropriate:

> *Bear with me and let me be. If you get tired of listening to me talk, don't listen, but don't let me know you're not listening. I'm so confused, I hurt so much. Will you just let me cry and hang in there with me? Hold my hand while I go through it? Don't try to make sense out of it and don't give me advice.*

If we have the courage to offer our friends gentle but clear messages of what we need, the results may be mutually beneficial. And for those who are not able to respond to such a request, remember that we have other needs and they have other skills.

## *Getting On With Life*—One noteworthy dimension of bereavement is that, after the first few weeks, many of us are doing two things simultaneously. We are experiencing our grief all, or most, of the time while we return to our daily routine, including work, family responsibilities, the details of settling affairs, etc.

Having a life to manage and responsibilities to see to is a very good refuge for many. Tom puts it simply,

"… maybe I grieve on the inside while doing business on the outside."

Elizabeth has two wonderful metaphors to describe her state of mind.

*Sometimes when you put a glass in the dishwasher, it fractures. My theory is that if you knock the glass against the faucet in picking it up, you fracture it invisibly. It looks intact, but when you put it in the dishwasher it falls apart. I've thought of myself in that way, like a glass that had a severe jolt that doesn't show, but is more vulnerable now. I mean, I really felt I had been okay and now I was not necessarily fully okay.*

• • •

*We had a grandfather clock that didn't run, so we just stood it up. Our clock man looked at it and said that was an example of atavism. He said that when an elephant dies, its fellow elephants handle the death by propping it up so it looks alive. I think grief is like that for a while. You look more functional than you really are.*

We are propped up by the people around us and/or the circumstances of our daily routine. Propped up or not, we can't grieve continuously, so the business of functioning effectively in tandem with doing our grief work is a sound, healthy procedure.

Sarah had some wonderful words of hope for coping during those days.

*No matter how tough things get, I never lose hope. Never quit, never, never quit. Some good things come from it...You're more aware of what can happen, so you find greater joy in little things each day.*

*Life must go on. You never forget the one you've lost, but the living are more important now. We take one day at a time, live it as well as we can and somehow the healing happens. I've learned to be thankful for the time I had with Michelle and the precious time I have with my children now.*

*Good-Byes*—In a suicide death, we are usually deprived of the opportunity to say good-bye. Our loved one had the last word, leaving us with all the unfinished business of our relationship.

For that reason, it may be important to have that conversation you were denied. Guided by our counselor, Bob and I created such an opportunity. We each wrote Cathy a letter shortly after her death. Bob's letter came fairly easily, but mine was a terribly laborious undertaking. I spent long hours at my typewriter and cried a great many tears.

We also went to the columbarium where Cathy's ashes are interred. It was two hours away so we didn't go on a regular basis but, when we were nearby, we usually stopped. It was a time for us to reminisce about her and others who are interred there, to say a prayer and to have some private moments as well.

Barbara had two visions right after her son's suicide that had a powerful force in her grief work and her ability to say good-bye.

> *I was sitting at the kitchen table listening to the conversation of gathered family and friends, when this vision just penetrated. I saw Gary going into a tunnel filled with light. Clear, bright light. That probably was a very critical moment in my survival early on.*

The second occurred while she and her family were sitting in the limousine after the funeral:

> *Here I am, feeling like it's absolutely the end of the world, and I keep looking for Gary and can't find him anywhere. Suddenly, I have a vision of my son turning somersaults in a weightless environment. And he's shouting, 'Wheee!' Like, 'Hey, it's fun here. It's OK, Mom.'*

Barbara sensed that Gary was asking her to let him go, that he needed freedom and so did she. Somehow it released them both.

You will recognize your good-bye when it happens. I hope you will feel a certain sense of closure and that it will enable you to move along in your new life somewhat more peacefully.


*Guilt*—One story speaks eloquently of guilt. An older couple knew his brother was suicidal and that he'd been hospitalized for previous attempts. He called to express suicidal thoughts again, and they jumped immediately into their car and raced over to his house. They were too late.

The couple's guilt was overwhelming. He relates,

> *We couldn't even look each other in the eye for weeks and we still can't talk about it. It's like it happened yesterday, even though it was several years ago. But, it seems to help to tell you, to sort of get if off my chest.*

The lesson is explicit. Given his brother's determination, he would almost certainly have completed suicide sooner or later. It simply would have been impossible for them to continuously intervene.

He says, "That's what gets me through the nights. Since he was that determined, I have to believe that he's found his peace. Now I have to find mine."

Suicide deaths often leave a legacy of guilt. There may be a nagging suspicion that they committed suicide because of some failure on our part. We assume that others are likewise attaching blame to us which, of course, compounds our guilt.

Guilt notwithstanding, we must keep reminding ourselves that it was our loved one who made the choice. With the possible exception of those whose quality of life was unbearable, our wish would have been otherwise and we are monumentally saddened by their decision.

There are infinite dimensions of guilt. One woman felt guilty because she didn't tell her father she loved him the last time she saw him. Another described feeling responsible for her mother's death because she hadn't been a good enough daughter. One father's guilt took a bizarre twist when he learned that his deceased son's friends dealt their parents the unthinkable cruelty of threatening suicide to get what they wanted.

There is one universal dimension, however. We all brought something less than perfection to our relationship with our loved one. Imbedded in my own guilt was the keen awareness that I was, without question, an imperfect mother. At first my shortcomings took on exaggerated dimension. In time I understood that there is no such thing as a "perfect parent."

One friend listened to my lamentation and responded with a comment I will never forget: "Cathy is not dead because you made mistakes as a parent." I learned that my weaknesses were human but, in my case, the difference was a double whammy. I not only never had the chance to tell Cathy I was sorry, I had overlaid them onto her suicide.

Mistakes or not, the day I learned to believe that I was not responsible for Cathy's decision was the day I began to recover.

I also had to learn that, given what I knew at the time, I had done everything I could think of to do to help my daughter. Now, of course, I would make changes were I fortunate enough to revisit life with her.

But wisdom is cumulative and, at any given point, we are only as wise as the lessons our life experiences enable us to be. And, in any case, we'll never know whether doing things differently might have prevented the suicide.

We often call them the "If Onlys." We replay them over and over again. It is an exercise in futility that we live with as long as we choose to, and it does have the power to hold us hostage.

## Bill

Bill has a wonderful approach to the concept of guilt that has served him well during his grief journey. He is a health professional who retired nine days after his son, Van, first attempted suicide. As a single parent, Bill raised four of his five children from early childhood. Van was 22 and living at home. Late one evening, he stabbed himself in the throat and chest. When Bill discovered him, he took him to the ER where he was treated and then admitted.

Van was diagnosed paranoid-schizophrenic and placed on medication and subsequently discharged into his father's care. For the next nine months, Bill watched helplessly while Van struggled with his illness at the same time that he continued to work and maintain some semblance of a normal life.

*It's hard to know what's going on in the mind of a crazed person, but I know that his overriding fear was spending his life in jail and that's where his paranoia was rampant.*

*Rather than going to jail, he concluded that
he would prefer to die. An inner drive
seemed to leave him no choice. He was
trying to solve that problem and eventually
he did.*

Van completed suicide that same year.

*He went to a movie that night with his
sister, Allison. They came home and talked.
Then she went home and he got in his car
and drove out into the country. There was a
slight downhill grade and he went very fast
and ran his car directly into a large stone
boulder.*

*Before his illness, Van was doing very
well. He was handsome, he was into body
building, he was outgoing, he was self-
confident and he had saved some money. He
had plans for a great life and was on his
way.*

*He changed dramatically as a result of
his illness. I guess some schizophrenics
progress slowly, but in his case, it was
sudden.*

For Bill, the distinction between regret and
guilt is clear. Regrets are part of the human
condition, but there would be no guilt for events
over which he had no control.

*Van's suicide was a result of his illness,
so I've never had the first guilt feeling. I
wouldn't change anything. I was a loving
father, I gave him plenty of emotional
support and I can't think of anything that I
would do differently.*

Give your imagination free rein to address your guilt as you need to and then, with equal dedication, examine all the arguments that refute it. The sooner done, the better, because guilt has nothing constructive to contribute to this experience.

***Healing*—**Healing is our destination, but when we arrive there are no bells or whistles. We get there a day at a time. Lois has an earthy description for it, "You don't pick the scab off and it's bleeding again; it's just a dull ache that's there all the time."

Implicit in healing is the reality that there will be occasional times when we're overwhelmed again. What's different is that we're not incapacitated as we are early on and our relapse is brief.

### *Doug and Karen*
Doug and his wife, Karen, lost their son, Brad, to suicide at the age of 24. Brad was an introverted child.

Doug relates, *He would get anxiety attacks. When we took him to college, he had such an attack that he left his room and went to the car. He was a nervous wreck. We think he was agoraphobic—afraid of being with people.*

Brad's academic accomplishments were legendary.

*He was one of 11 high school juniors chosen nationwide to work at the Jackson Laboratory on genetic mice cancer. He did a*

*summer internship at Harvard and another
at Columbia and he successfully challenged
an error in a math textbook. He graduated
Phi Beta Kappa and Summa Cum Laude in
geophysics and Harvard gave him a fellow-
ship for graduate work.*

*Socially he struggled so, but academi-
cally he went off the graphs. He was an
announcer at his college radio station, but
when someone came to the house, he disap-
peared. He didn't want to meet anyone.*

The week Brad died, the family had gone to
their cottage on the Cape and they asked Brad to
join them. Doug talked to him on Thursday and
suggested he come on down to meet them and
Brad indicated that he would.

*So, I was surprised not to find him
there. Jill, (Brad's sister) went home that
evening and Brad was there. They talked,
and then he went hiking in the woods and
Jill came down to the Cape. She said Brad
was going up to Maine. Jill got home first
on Sunday and she found him sitting on the
couch downstairs. He had shot himself.*

Shortly after Brad's death, Doug, a third
generation building contractor, began a new
puttering activity. It started by chance, the way
things often do but, as time went on, it became
quite engaging, and then it became compelling.

*About three weeks after Brad died, I
went out to the corral and began picking up
rocks and putting them in buckets. I picked
all the rocks up and filled 50 or 60 of those
white 5 gallon buckets and brought them
down to the Cape. There's a 50 foot stretch*

*out back that was a big bank covered with briars, and I started dumping the buckets of rocks there.*

*Over three years, it's grown and grown...I've made an area about 40 feet by 40 feet. Now the lawn goes right to the marsh. I know my neighbor thinks I'm nuts, but it has kept me sane. I bring 30 or 40 buckets at a time and dump them. I've planted grass and evergreens, but I've done it all a few buckets at a time.*

*Maybe psychologically or subconsciously it's a memorial. I never thought of it that way. After Brad died, I didn't want to do anything important.*

This project, affectionately know in the family as "doing buckets" has provided a splendid, ongoing, permanent improvement to their beach property at the same time that it has offered Doug a therapeutic focus to relieve the pressures of work and grief. And, it is a living memorial to his son. It doesn't get any more healing than that.

The wonder of healing also is that the means are as varied as the personalities of the survivors. Some take on projects, some become involved in support groups, some change careers and relocate, some look inward.

The determination to honor Cathy's bidding to get on with our lives compelled us to make our peace with her decision. Also, I believe she never lost the will to live so much as she lost the strength, and she trusted that we would understand. It made the choice easy: there was none.

Elizabeth's musical metaphor portrays it well. Before the death of our loved one, we live in the key of C Major, a bright, vibrant key. We feel in charge, the music of our lives is joyous.

After suicide that is forever transformed. We will dance again, but not for awhile and, as she puts it, "…now it's in a minor key. It is lovely, but it's different. We're all permanently changed."

## *Helplessness*—Another legacy of suicide is helplessness. If we didn't know our loved one was hurting, why didn't we? Or, maybe we knew and did everything we could think of, yet the suicide left us feeling that we didn't do enough.

### *Renée*

Renée lost her brother, Peter, five years ago. She last saw Peter on her wedding day six months prior to his death.

*One good thing happened two weeks before the wedding. Peter and I took a walk around the block and, we were having such a great conversation that we walked around four times. In that way, I kind of got my good-byes in that nobody else really did.*

Peter was a high school senior. One evening he was studying in his room and his dad was downstairs when he heard an odd noise. He said it sounded like someone knocked books off the desk. Peter had shot himself.

Why would Peter choose to end his life so prematurely?

Renée says, *Everyone came to different conclusions, but I know he was thinking of it before I got married. Nine months before my wedding he said, 'I'm going to tell you something if you promise not to tell.' I promised and he told me that he'd tried to commit suicide. He drank and took pills and was surprised when he woke up. I asked whether he felt he might try again, and he said 'No.' He said he thought it was stupid but he may have said that because he knew I'd worry.*

There is one regret which troubles Renée.

*I wish I'd known Peter was so depressed. He was sleeping a lot, but I didn't know why. Looking back, it makes sense. I wish I could have stopped it. I wish I'd known what to do, but I didn't. Maybe you always wish you could have done something to stop it.*

One mother read her son's journal after his suicide and was shocked. She lamented, "It is inconceivable to me that my son could have been in so much pain, could have had so many demons and I simply had no idea that that was the case."

Bill speaks of his feelings of helplessness: "… this was one of the most difficult, frustrating, disappointing things I had to face. I could not help my son and, most of the time I was fearful."

Helplessness challenges us to differentiate between those dimensions of our loved one's life that were within our power to influence and those that were not. We cannot know what someone chooses not to share, nor are we at fault because we are not omnipotent. Perhaps our best defense against helplessness is to take the reins of our life more diligently than ever before.

*Holidays*–Holidays are special days with abundant memories. The empty chair always seems emptier as our memories bring in clear focus the absence of our loved one.

The first year is exceptionally difficult. Be gentle with yourself. Give your plans careful thought and don't do anything that will put you in an emotional bind. If the thought of a Christmas tree sounds too difficult, don't put one up. If your loved one always made mincemeat pie for Thanksgiving, plan to have strawberry mousse this year. If the special Menorah that the family lit together is filled with too many memories, buy a new one.

One person said that when she felt herself sinking, she would go to bed and eat ice cream and Christmas cookies. Another said eating peanut butter sandwiches and popcorn helped him get through some of those inevitable moments.

Giving yourself permission to make changes in your holiday traditions and rituals is an excellent way to moderate those times, and it embodies a subtle and valuable by-product. You will establish new traditions that may be comforting in future years.

The first Christmas after Cathy's death, we wrestled with the issue of stockings on the mantle. I had made hers when she was an infant, so there was great attachment to it. I wasn't ready to leave it in the box, not so soon after her death and knowing that Christmas was her favorite holiday.

I discussed it with Bob and our sons. I said that, with their permission, I wanted to hang it up. They agreed and the matter was settled. It was the right thing to do that year and, as a result, I was able to throw it away and make new stockings for everyone the following year.

A new tradition with amazing healing quality began for me that first holiday. The previous year I had made a few little red knitted bells, and Cathy thought they were wonderful. Shortly after her death, I found myself making them in earnest.

I stopped counting when I reached the 1,000 mark, and they have gone to an ever-widening love network around the world. The response is heartwarming. Some let me know year after year how they enjoy their bells. One couple placed theirs permanently on a kitchen cupboard. Another took theirs to the Bahamas to add to a tree of shells and seaweed. My mom passed them out to her caregivers, who asked for more. I felt like a proverbial knitting machine, but I loved it! One Jewish friend put hers on a stabile that hangs over the fireplace, another hangs his on his refrigerator.

Go with your instincts at holiday time—whatever they may be. Be open and communicative about your feelings. You may discover some comforting surprises along the way.

## *Loneliness/Isolation*—The feelings of loneliness and isolation associated with suicide, as we can all attest, are beyond description. We probably don't know anyone who has experienced it and we sense, with good reason, that others cannot truly understand our pain.

We may unwittingly exacerbate the situation by not talking about it. The effect of our silence may be to erect a wall that increases both our isolation and our friends' discomfort. The choice to endure this experience alone will create a significant additional burden to live with.

Friends were a problem issue for Barbara. As the grieving person doesn't know how to handle her pain, friends often don't know how to handle their grieving companion.

*If you have cancer, your friends care a lot but what can they do for you? The same with death. My friends didn't know whether to try to cheer me up or tell me how I really looked or tell me I looked great. They simply didn't know how to handle it and neither did I.*

*One of my friends had just lost her mother to cancer and she was living alone. Another friend*

*had just gone through a divorce, so all of our lives
had suddenly and dramatically changed.*

Her friends interpreted Barbara's withdrawal as an
indication that she was trying to break it off with them, a
feeling they finally confessed two years later.

*They thought I didn't want to be around them.
The truth is, I didn't know how to be with myself—
how could I know how to be around anyone else?*

Occasionally, we are fortunate when someone comes
forward to tell us of their own experience. They are angels
of mercy! As one woman said, "Suicide is something that
people don't talk about much. Every time someone did, in
one case after hiding it for years, it meant a great deal to
me." Such disclosures create an instant brotherhood and
the modeling opportunity that follows is a singular gift.

Don't be shy. Share your feelings with the people
around you. Accept and gratefully acknowledge every
gesture of friendship and support that is offered. Do whatever comes to mind that you think may reduce your
isolation.

I work at home which is lonely at times. Following
Cathy's death I learned to compensate. When loneliness
took over, I would set my work aside and go shopping,
wander through a mall, visit with salespersons. I often
invented errands that would put me in touch with the world
around me.

Sometimes I called a friend. That was problematic in my case because my network was scattered across the country. Though I somehow restrained myself, I could have done severe damage to our phone budget during those early months.

Correspondence is something I enjoy and I learned that pouring my feelings out to friends was exceptionally therapeutic. One generous friend became an enduring pen pal during those lonely years. I am eternally in her debt for the sensitivity she showed in responding faithfully and quickly to my letters. She even saved them and returned them when I began to write this book. I carefully maintained our written dialogue and did not alter it by phoning as she was the one person I knew who would remain an absolutely steadfast correspondent.

I struggled laboriously with loneliness. I not only knew no one who had been through a kidney transplant, I knew no one who had experienced suicide. I needed models desperately. People I could talk to...people who had been there, who would hug and encourage me...people who were on the road to recovery. When I learned of a group for survivors getting under way in my community, I looked forward eagerly and fearfully to attending the first meeting. That was a year-and-a-half after Cathy's death and it was an incredible relief. At last, I had acquired some traveling companions for my passage. My days were vastly improved by carrying those newfound friendships in my heart.

Barbara shares that another source of healing for her was SOS, a self-help group (see Support Groups for more information) that she helped organize and lead. "I think the most valuable thing I've learned that could help another person through this journey would be to offer them the support of fellow travelers such as the people in SOS."

## *Measuring Progress*—Measuring progress is an all-important exercise. Anniversaries and holidays can be useful to us in this context. It requires extra effort, but making notes in a journal or diary on anniversaries or holidays may not only be therapeutic, it provides an important frame of reference for future use.

Our favorite time of the year can also be a benchmark. Spring, when the earth comes to life again, is my favorite, but I thought I would lose my mind that first spring after Cathy's death. Watching the bulbs come up again when my daughter was not coming back to life was torture. But, the second spring was a little easier, and gradually I learned to look forward to it again. It is the time for indulging in a passion of mine, working in the garden. I have also discovered that I often feel close to Cathy when I'm digging in the soil. Maybe my mind is relaxed and this invites reflection and promotes spiritual receptivity.

Another yardstick occurred when I attended a reunion with some college friends. We had gathered four years earlier at my home, so the memories were vivid. I was amazed by the difference. At the first one I was still crippled. The next time I was quite sound, certainly not the same person I was before, but solid and strong. I understood it and they validated it. It was a moment of great reassurance.

As Doug related, the experience of a neighbor had considerable bearing on his thoughts about a timetable.

*When he lost his boy, I think it took him about three years to heal. So, in my mind, I'm saying 'three years'. Well, three years has come and gone and I'm still not totally there. Not feeling super.*

*And, then, someone said six years, so I'm saying, 'Geez, maybe I'm halfway there.' I don't know, but I'm much better than I was. I've improved but I'm still in pain sometimes, and I expect to have that feeling at times for as long as I live. I can't imagine losing that pain totally.*

The important thing is to be aware of the direction of your passage. As Renée said, "You know what terrible shape you were in at year one. Now, it's almost five years and, at that point, you know you're going to be in a very different place than you were four years ago."

If you are—congratulations! If not, take heed of where you would like to make improvements and go for it.


*Memories*—Memories are an important dimension of our recovery, but often not in the beginning. At first, they tend to evoke heartache and intensify the feelings of loss. They are relentlessly heightened by anniversaries, holidays and all the special times that bring to mind our loved one.

But, there is more to be said about memories. For one thing, we don't want them to become disabling. Tom dis-

cusses his feelings about the subway after his son completed suicide by jumping in front of one.

> *When Margaret and Betsy went to Scott's
> apartment after his death, they rode the subway.
> That bugged me for awhile. How in the world was
> I going to face another subway? I often wondered
> how it would be for someone to jump in front of a
> train.*

> *But, I never saw another subway until we
> went to Paris three years later. And then, we did
> have reason to use one. I felt pretty
> squeamish...It's something I can't get out of my
> mind—picturing him jumping in front of the train.
> But, I'm not going to worry about it. I did face the
> subway, and I rode it a lot more after that. I don't
> know whether it would have been better if I'd
> faced it six months afterward instead of three
> years later.*

Photographs are a tough issue. My husband spent
hours examining our family photo albums the day after
Cathy's death. I couldn't look at them for several years.
Tom takes special comfort in a favorite photo of Scott on
vacation with them. Doug, on the other hand, can't look at
the photos of Brad sitting around their house.

Although our loved ones chose to die, we surely do
not want them to be remembered for that reason. Rather,
we want people to remember the joys of knowing them and
the contributions they made during their lifetime.

As time passes, there is significant therapeutic value in happy memories. It is empowering in the grief experience to take charge of the quality of our memories.

Tom's approach is remarkable. He makes a point of referring to his cherished memories whenever possible. "If there's a time in conversations when I want to mention Scott, I don't hesitate. I'll say, 'I remember Scott used to like to do this,' or 'Scott and I used to do such and such.' It makes me feel good to talk about him."

*Relocation/Travel*–Whether it is a short trip or an extended vacation, getting away can be an effective respite from our grief work—a way to shore ourselves up for the next round. But, we need to remember that relief is short-lived. When we return, our grief will be awaiting us. If we approach it as such, travel can be beneficial. If we regard it as a cure-all, we are in for a disappointment.

Relocation can likewise be an effective change, whether across town, across state or across country. If your loved one wasn't living with you, a move might have a somewhat different meaning, but, in any case, it can be quite restorative.

I have tested all of the above and discovered that each has merit. Several months after Cathy's death, I spent two weeks visiting Dave in Texas and old friends in Chapel Hill. It was my first visit to Dave's college world. The mother in me very badly needed to see his environment, meet his friends, watch him play basketball, be sure that he was okay. In addition, I needed to return to Chapel Hill to cry with Cathy's friends and to revisit our home and her horse facilities there. I sorely missed the comfort of my old friends. They enveloped me in their collective embrace, and did I ever need it.

We experienced relocation as well. Thankfully, we had moved from Cathy's childhood home prior to her death. Then we moved from our rental house a year, almost to the day, after her death. I hoped it would be beneficial because it was time to move forward.

It was beneficial, but not until I faced some tough issues. While our rented house was not Cathy's childhood home, it was the last house we shared with her. It felt as though we had left her in some intangible way that I was unable to articulate.

I have a poignant memory of that event. As we organized the den in our new home, Bob hung a favorite portrait of Cathy riding sidesaddle prominently behind the television. Then he sat back in his chair, looked at it awhile, and said, "There, Cathy, here we are in our new home." Then we both cried. In that moment was born the reality that from then and forever more, we would live in our home—any home—without her.

Also a task awaited me after our move that took on a degree of difficulty I could not have imagined. When we arrived, I was faced with dozens of boxes that had been stored in the attic in our rental house. Every time I opened another box, I found something that reminded me of Cathy.

It triggered memory upon memory. In the process, I became fairly dysfunctional all over again. It took perhaps two months, but, what felt like two lifetimes, to get through those boxes.

Nonetheless, it clearly was in the best interest of all of us to be in a new home, one we had not shared with Cathy. A home where we could build new memories as our life without her continued.

There are valid arguments on both sides of making a move. Some people need the solid feeling of roots and a family home that withstands the test of time. For some, it is easier to be in a physically different place than the home we occupied during our loved one's life. Moving to a new community may offer the additional stimulation of new surroundings, new beginnings.

Whatever your decision, be sure you have taken ample time to think it through carefully and with full knowledge of your reasons and expectations for staying or going.

*Self-Protection*—Suicide changes everything. Life, as we knew it, is no more. We put on a new and very different pair of glasses. And we recognize, perhaps for the first time, that all of us are at risk.

Elizabeth speaks about this.

*I might have done less career-wise than I would have without the suicide, simply because family became an even higher priority. Also, my*

*sense of optimism about how things work out was
severely damaged. I no longer have the same
feeling that things will end happily. There is not
the same kind of safety anymore.*

The changes in our assumptions may significantly impact on our lives. For many, our willingness to take risks may be impaired. We may become more conservative. We have learned that an ordinary life can be torn asunder at any moment and we know with absolute certainty how crippling it can be.

Thus, we protect ourselves and this may become a powerful motivation to simplify our world. We are more intentional about doing things in a way that will safeguard us.

In retrospect, I can see that we reacted predictably to our losses. We had not only lost our daughter, we had, in entirely different terms, lost our beloved David two years earlier to his collegiate world so far away. Our youngest son, Tim, was the only child still in the nest. With the best of intentions, we closed circle around him. I know we made his passage to manhood considerably more difficult, even though he executed it with characteristic grace. I hope he has forgiven us our well-meaning transgressions.

It is constructive to develop protective mechanisms that will help us, but they must not become disabling. Loey's message that "Hurts have taught me never to give up loving," addresses this point. There is always the possibility of losing another loved one, but our lives would be vastly diminished were we to choose not to love again "just in case."


## *Shock*—Shock is indispensable.

It kicks in without our consent the moment we learn of our loved one's suicide. It is short-lived, lasting for a few days or weeks. It enables us to carry out our immediate responsibilities with surprising poise while we are fundamentally in a stupor.

Doug Manning aptly describes grief with this metaphor:

> *Grief is like an onion. It comes off one layer at a time and you cry a lot.*

> *As you peel the onion, the first layer you encounter is the thin, papery like outer skin. It comes off in your hand and crumbles like confetti. If you threw it up in the air, it would swirl around before landing.*

> *The shock stage of grief is like that—a multitude of emotions, questions, tasks to be done—all swirling around our heads. Some may land for a moment and we might start a thought, but they will soon blow away again and we can't remember what we were saying.*


## *Stigma*—Stigma is often, but not always, a by-product of suicide.

If we are stigmatized or embarrassed by it, we surely will travel a more hazardous road to wellness.

This legacy may even transcend generations.

### *JoAnne*

JoAnne's daughter, Katy, age 25, completed suicide by hanging herself. She had been hospitalized several years earlier and her diagnosis, not disclosed to her mother at the time, was schizophrenia. Her psychiatrist told JoAnne later that Katy was one of the most disturbed patients he had ever treated.

JoAnne's father had completed suicide when she was 21, but her mother never told her how he died.

*She's never talked about it to this day. He died on her birthday. She said he wanted to give her her freedom. She called me and said, 'Your father died,' and I went home and cried and went around like I didn't know what this was all about.*

*I read in the newspaper that he shot himself. We lived in the country and we had chickens, so he had several guns. He retired when I was 11 and we moved to Minnesota and then he became alcoholic, depressed and abusive. My mom ran a guest house that barely made ends meet, and she had an awful time dealing with him during those years.*

With such a legacy of stigma, JoAnne might have faced a major stumbling block in her grief work. But she was fortunate to have a job in a mental health clinic at the time of Katy's suicide. Her superiors and co-workers were

understanding and supportive, and her friends
were compassionate.

> *I didn't feel put down at all, or any*
> *criticism, or that it was something to hide.*
> *It just never hit me that way at work or*
> *anywhere else. Everybody knew about*
> *Katy's attempt five years earlier. This was*
> *just—she had done it, that's all. It was just*
> *the unbelievable shock that she had done it.*

Elizabeth is a physician and she is married to
a physician. "We learned about people who lost
loved ones to suicide and grieving and reacting to
loss..." Because she lives in the medical world,
stigma likewise played no part in her experience.

Whether we experience stigma—the shame, the accu-
sations, the attachment of suicide to the family—seems to
be, in part, a function of the people around us. If those in
our network recognize that suicide is not about the survivors, but about the victim, we will not feel it.

Some survivors, however, sense the presence of stigma
even when it isn't actually articulated. There may be an
underlying feeling that people think something is wrong
with the family. One woman said she didn't tell anyone
about her father's suicide for five years. One man said he
felt that people blamed the family because his father died by
suicide. One woman related a friend's comment at the
wake. He said, "See, I hope you're happy for what you've
done." Several others walked past her and the coffin and
didn't speak.

Sarah's response is stirring,

> *...if people felt a stigma, I felt sorrier for*
> *them than for myself.  I felt badly that they*
> *couldn't acknowledge that suicide happens and*
> *that it won't necessarily touch them.  To hide*
> *behind fear is so much more devastating to them.*

Those of us who experience stigma can, like Sarah, do
something about it.  While we have no control over what
people think or say, we do control our own feelings.  Here
again is where a sensitive friend or a good therapist may be
able to assist us.  Discussing it with someone who under-
stands the issue can be invaluable.

## *Support Groups*—For many survivors, one of the
most useful activities is participation in a support group.
They meet bi-weekly or monthly to share the pain,
struggles, progress and setbacks unique to the experiences
of suicide survivors.

A support group serves as a frame of reference.  It
provides us with models, with suggestions and ideas about
how others have dealt with this experience.  A support group
confirms our feelings and validates much of what is happening to us. Most of all, it reduces the loneliness.

One person summed it up well.

> *Nobody in the world has lived with such*
> *pain.  And I didn't know how I would ever get*
> *through it, or how I would get through the rest of*

*my life. Somebody has got to help me. I even wondered whether I was going crazy, and if the things I was feeling and the things I was doing were normal, or off-the-wall or what. When I heard others saying the same things I was feeling, that helped me see that what I was experiencing was pretty much like everyone else.*

Another person states,

*You can't really get going with your life until you've gone through the grief. To be able to sit there and listen to other people who have gone through it can actually start someone's grief process, even though it might be two, three, four years down the line.*

Attending group meetings is not an easy thing to do. It requires a lot of courage to sit for two hours and listen to the suffering in the room. Every story is sad and it is painful to hear some of the terrible experiences others have endured. We may find it difficult to imagine ourselves living with some of the circumstances that are shared.

One person said, "Sometimes I come home feeling worse for listening to someone else's tragic story. But, at the same time, so many survivors are truly heroic, and it validates this awful experience in a way that nothing else does."

At first it may be difficult to say aloud that our loved one completed suicide. The encouragement of a support group can be immensely important in helping us verbalize our experience and feelings.

Self-help groups include survivors who are in various stages of recovery. Some are years down the road and making visible progress. Some are years down the road and only now addressing their grief. Some talk a lot, others speak little. Some are newly bereaved and struggling to speak at all. Some need to share their story once or twice, others share different parts of it from meeting to meeting. Some need to repeat their story again and again. Some come once, some come occasionally, some come to every meeting until they are ready to move on in their lives.

In his book, ***The Gift of Significance***, Doug Manning writes "People are not going to move forward in their grief until the significance of the person who has died has been established. People who can establish significance, make progress. Those who cannot do so, hang on and hurt."

Thus it is that we can help one another no matter where we are in our recovery. We can listen to each other's stories as we strive to establish the significance of the person we lost, as well as the significance of the event that has turned our lives upside down.

Even veterans continue to learn and grow while adding, by their presence and their courage, a tangible message of hope. They are giving back to the newly bereaved a little of what they received. Truly it is a full circle.

If you want to locate a support group in your area, consult a therapist, doctor, clergyperson, social services agency, library or newspaper.

There are also national organizations that maintain directories of local chapters/groups:

**American Association of Suicidology**
4201 Connecticut Avenue, NW #408
Washington, DC 20008
202-237-2280

**American Foundation for Suicide Prevention**
120 Wall Street, 22$^{nd}$ Floor
New York, NY 10005
888-333-2377

**Survivors of Suicide (SOS)**
locally organized but may be listed with one of
the above organizations.

**The Compassionate Friends**
active international organization for those who
have lost a child.
PO Box 3696
Oak Brook, IL 60522
630-990-0010

**The Samaritans**
Greater New York area
PO Box 1259
Madison Square Station
New York, NY 10159
emergency 24-hour hot line
212-673-3000

Boston area
500 Commonwealth Avenue
Boston, MA    02215
617-247-0220 or 617-536-2460

If you are unsuccessful in locating a support group in your community, start one! Any of these organizations will gladly help you get underway. Barbara will tell you, as she organized and became a co-leader of an SOS group in her community, "What was unexpected is what I got in return. Hearing about the incredibly heroic work that other people have done is one of the most important things I've gained from SOS."

*Timetable*—In my experience the business of grief following a loved one's suicide, if we sign up for it in the beginning, is minimally a two-year process. Understanding that we never stop grieving entirely, but the threshold we reach—from on-going intense pain to a more softened, dull ache—occurs at around the two-year mark *for most people.*

That time frame is, of course, subject to the profuse variations that constitute humankind. If we elect to set our grief work aside until we have the time or the strength to take it on, or if we choose to postpone it indefinitely or permanently, this timetable will not apply.

Sarah, Barbara and JoAnne, for valid reasons, postponed their grief work. Barbara's life had fallen apart on a variety of levels—divorce, new job, new town, son's suicide—and she knew it was imperative to protect herself carefully from facing it all at once.

Sarah's life and agenda took an unexpected twist when her grandsons were severely burned three months following her daughter's suicide. Thus, her time and attention were focused on their immediate needs for several months.

JoAnne was the Business Director of a pediatric psychiatric clinic. She felt really needed at work, the hours were flexible and she did not know what she would have done at home. So, she sidestepped her grief work to continue at the clinic, ". . .but I did that consciously because I felt I needed to finish this job before I could get on with the next." The key word is "consciously." JoAnne recognized that postponing her grief work meant just that. She would give it her full attention after retiring from the clinic.

In most cases, the best way to achieve a healthy outcome is to address your grief from the beginning. If you do, you can expect the first year to be a very long one. And, just when you think you're making headway, along comes the first anniversary. It brings the suicide event back into full focus as though it happened yesterday.

As Elizabeth says, ". . .the truth is that a year doesn't do for you all that you wish it would. It would be nice if you could squash your grief into one year and slam the door!"

For me, the first year seemed like endless days and nights of sadness and suffering. About a month after Cathy died, I visited with a most understanding woman who had lost her son to suicide seven years earlier. I will not forget her gentle injection of reality into my crippled life. She told me that the pain certainly does pass, but it takes a very long time. She said that not a day had passed in those seven years that she hadn't thought about her son and his suicide. It was a devastating prospect, but I soon understood that her kindly wisdom was meant to alert me to the reality of the challenges ahead.

Though I confess I didn't anticipate it, the second year was likewise very tough. Even though there were a great many times during that year when I became quasi-disabled again, I was also well aware that I was making progress. The second anniversary was every bit as painful as the first, but after that it did begin to get easier. At last, as Renée says, I knew the trend was in the right direction.

A lifelong friend, on approximately the fifth anniversary of Cathy's death, said to me one lazy afternoon while we were floating on the lake that she felt I was my cheerful old self again. I was at once encouraged by the glimpse of myself through her knowledgeable eyes, and stunned because I knew otherwise.

Little by little, I understood what her words were really saying. She was conveying her love as well as her innocence. It was her wish, and it reflected her comfort, to see the "old me" once again.

But, it was not so. In actuality, I would never again be that person. Still, there was a subtle and powerful suggestion in her message. That I appeared to her to be the person she knew before Cathy's death, offered heartening possibilities. I could approximate that person or, better yet, make some improvements. I accepted the latter as a promising challenge.

One gentleman describes his timetable. Because he delayed his grief work, it took him ten years, and a lot of therapy, to take a very important step forward. His mother was buried, at her request, where she was raised in a tiny town in northern Colorado. He describes going to this isolated place to visit her grave ten years later. It was there where he was able to process his feelings at last. Feelings that he had dared not confront all those years.

The world and the well-meaning people around you may do their best to impose a timetable on your grief work. Do yourself a favor. Nod politely to your generous advisors and go on about doing it in your own season.

*Tools*—The following is a brief list of some things survivors have done to assist them in their grief and recovery. They are offered merely as a starting point. The idea is to spend your time wisely and engage in meaningful activity as soon as possible. Above all, take good care of yourself. Do the necessary things, of course, and also find time to do things that make you feel good.

| | | |
|---|---|---|
| Exercise | Hobbies | Volunteer |
| Read | Learn a new skill | Pursue educational |
| Travel | Spend time with friends | studies |
| Pets | Art/Music | Religious activity |
| Crafts | Sports | |

*Understanding*—Some of us understand why our loved one chose suicide. The victim either left a note or his/her life circumstances made the decision self-explanatory. Some of us may even have been involved in the decision. Others do not know why it happened. There was no note or the note was not enlightening and the circumstantial evidence provided no clues.

It may be easier for those who understand the suicide to move forward. Without understanding, it will take a leap of faith to achieve acceptance.

First, it sends us off in search of the "whys." Looking for answers to explain our loved one's decision to die can become an obsession. We go over and over the details. We take it apart and put it together in endless combinations. We look for clues everywhere.

It's a little like solving a crime. Indeed, it may seem like a crime. The tragic irony, of course, is that the only person who can solve this crime is the person who perpetrated it.

The hypothesis we formulate may satisfy us for awhile. Then we think of another dimension that changes it, and off we go in search of the "whys" again.

There are times when we may rationalize that we did everything possible for our loved one, so the "whys" are not relevant. There are other times when our hearts play a different tune, and we're off again to resume our search.

After we have exhausted every hunch, innuendo and clue we can imagine, broken it down into every conceivable hypothesis, one of two things happens. Either we find an answer that we can live with, or we decide to accept the reality that we will never know why it happened and it's time to end the mind game and carry on.

The search for the "whys" may have origins beyond our need to understand our loved one's suicide. The more guilt we feel, the more energetic our search is likely to be.

As to suicide notes, they are often of great comfort to the survivors, but only a relatively small number of victims leave them. We were fortunate to have Cathy's note. It articulated her despair over her ongoing health complications and limited quality of life. The note, along with our awareness of her struggles, contributed much to our understanding. She had endured life-threatening surgery three times in her 23 years. When she learned that her kidneys had failed, she went immediately to the library and read the medical textbooks on dialysis and transplantation. She would have no false illusions about what lay ahead.

My sense is that Cathy didn't fear death. She was not a church-goer, but she read the Bible faithfully and talked about religion a lot. She had a strong belief in the life everlasting and she was spiritual in the broad and deep sense of the word. She was vivacious and happy-go-lucky, yes, but she was also a deep thinker.

Cathy was a horse trainer for several years and then she wanted to be a floor nurse. Both careers were out of reach for health reasons. I believe she was tormented by that. She was young and impatient and she had hoped transplantation would be the cure-all. While her kidney never rejected, she experienced a series of problems that sidelined her again and again. As her frustration increased, she seemed to have greater difficulty accepting her limitations.

A related issue alluded to earlier was that the considerable medications Cathy was taking following transplant were compromising her emotional well-being. She became increasingly and uncharacteristically anxious and distraught as time went on.

There was another important dimension of my understanding. As her mother, and as her kidney donor, I had intimate knowledge of the details of her health. Thus, I knew much about what she had gone through and that helped me through those long nights after her suicide. Because I was healthy and she was not, however, I also knew that my life experience allowed me to get only so close and then the door shut and she was alone with her poor health. Something I think we both understood.

Bill is thankful that his son's first suicide attempt clarified the nature of his illness. "If he had succeeded the first time, I never would have known why. I'm very grateful that I know why he did it."

Make every effort to understand your loved one's decision. If you cannot, consider the reasons why not. They may offer valuable insight. In either case, after a reasonable time, let it go so that this exercise does not become disabling. Reaching closure on this issue is essential to our progress.

**Well-Being**—If healing is our destination, well-being is our reward. But, it will not come quickly or easily. Nor will it be the same well-being we once enjoyed.

Some fortunate few of us may know from the start that we are going to be okay, that we will experience well-being again in the future. My guess is that at first, however, most of us question whether we will survive, much less reclaim that rewarding state of mind.

The people presented in this book have both illus-trated and persuaded you, I hope, that there is every possibility you will, in time, recover a meaningful and pleasurable sense of well-being. Their testimony is the best there is—direct personal experience.

The key is integration. Sooner or later, your pain will become integrated within your life tapestry so that you can resume life in a constructive and satisfying manner despite your loss.

Elizabeth offers another metaphor with respect to tragedy. She says,

> *In general, I like middle-aged people better than young people because they have been stepped on and trodden and pierced and punctured, and yet they are okay. Some young people have that dimension to them, usually because they have been through some unfortunate things. But, the totally unscathed people–I can admire them from a distance, but it's a little hard to relate to them*

*except as splendid animals cantering through a field.*

If we were "unscathed" before our loss, we have now joined what is probably the majority. Those who have been "pierced and punctured," whose lives include losses as well as gains. Most of them, nonetheless, view the world through a half-full glass. They epitomize the can-do philosophy. A positive attitude can contribute much to our ability to recover.

Another dimension that can assist us is dreaming of our loved one. Dreams are sometimes disturbing, but more often they are comforting and sometimes even liberating.

Lois had a dream about her brother, Rob, two months after he died and it was a very comforting experience. She writes:

*It was a wintry day, gray and gloomy. My dark, depressed mood was suddenly interrupted by the sound of light tapping on my kitchen door. I felt weak, and it took most of my energy just to walk to the door and open it. To my surprise, there stood Rob. He asked if he could come in.*

*'Of course, Rob, come in,' I said. 'I'm so happy to see you.' I was reluctant to break from the warmth of his hug, but I motioned him to sit down at the kitchen table while I turned to the stove to put on some coffee. When Rob came, it was always a nice, long visit. We would need a full pot of coffee.*

'Please don't bother with the coffee,' Rob said, 'I can only stay a few minutes.'

'A few minutes? Don't be silly, Rob. We have so much to talk about. I want to tell you how I feel. These past two months, I have felt cold and devastated. I can't eat or sleep; and when I'm alone, I cry all the time. Sometimes I go out for walks to clear my head, but nothing helps. I feel so alone. Can you help me, Rob? The pain is terrible.'

'You'll be okay,' he assured me, holding my cold hands in his. 'That's why I stopped by, to tell you that. In time, you'll be okay.'

'You sound so sure, Rob. How do you know that?'

'I just do. Now please trust me. You will be okay.' And, with a quick hug, he left.

I tried desperately to get him to stay, but he would only promise to come back if I needed him. I could hear my voice calling after him, 'I do need you, Rob. Come back!' His visit was too short, and I felt cheated. Why did he have to go so soon?

When I awoke from my dream of Rob, I truly felt his presence, and I realized that he was trying to help me with my pain. I knew then, that I would survive. I'm grateful for that dream—and for the chance to touch him once more. I felt as if Rob freed me to be myself. I'm doing things now that I might have held back on before.

Well-being may have spiritual dimensions, both in the narrow and the broad sense of the term. For me, there has been great comfort in believing that Cathy found her peace in the Heaven she envisioned. Still, she remains a part of me in a mystical way that I often feel but do not understand. She visits me in my dreams, she comes quickly to mind when I see people or things that remind me of her.

Feeling Cathy's spiritual presence was not sustaining in the beginning. But, I have suffered much and journeyed a long way and learned to take what I can get. I now know how to take comfort from the intangible and elusive nature of her spiritual presence in my life today.

Some people rely directly on their religious beliefs. Lois describes her view of it.

> *They talk about Heaven on earth. I think much of it is inside of us right here and now. I mean, if Heaven is really there, well, that's great, it'll be a wonderful bonus. But, if it isn't, we'd better enjoy all the best stuff we can while we're here. Why wait to find out what goes on afterwards!*

A sense of well-being is probably the "best stuff" of which Lois speaks. It is the best that we can hope for.

Seek and ye shall find.

# *FINAL THOUGHTS—*
# *MOUNTAIN CLIMBING*

Life is precious. That our loved ones completed suicide does nothing to negate the fact. They made the choice to forsake life, and their choice is, at once, our great loss and theirs.

It also offers us an unexpected opportunity. We have the balance of our life ahead of us and we have the choice to spend it as we will. Will we throw it away, drift along aimlessly, or choose to spend it wisely? For some the decision is formulated in the beginning; one way or the other it isn't a choice. For others it evolves gradually. But, consciously or unconsciously, willingly or unwillingly, each of us makes the decision.

Our discussions have been about the grief journey, about reconciling our pain. If we are to recover, we must sooner or later toil through the anguish of our loved one's suicide. We must weave it into the tapestry of our life.

In the final analysis, this experience has the distinct potential to widen and deepen our appreciation of life. It is a moment in time to discover that our spirit is more resilient than we ever imagined, that there is a life of quality before us that is ours for the asking.

I invite you to open your heart to the possibilities. Recognizing that it is a long journey and, keeping in mind all the while, that you can create your own passage to a fulfilling future. It requires that you pay close attention to what's happening to you, listen carefully to what you are feeling, decide where you are going, and seek reinforcements as you discover the need for them.

Your journey will not be a smooth one, any more than the road from New York to Montreal is straight and smooth. There are bumps, bends , occasional detours and the mighty Adirondack Mountains to climb. But, if you choose Montreal as your destination, don't be tempted to change course when you see a good-sized mountain ahead. Instead, make sure you have extra supplies—plenty of food, gas, good tires, maps, a compass and a survival kit. On an ambitious journey, it is wise to be prepared.

Getting well is a gallant undertaking. It is a journey from a dismal existence filled with sorrow to a gratifying life of achievement, contribution and joy. It is when your loved one's chair joins the landscape of your experience as a symbol of the life that was lived. It is an opportunity with abundant challenge and, I hope, irresistible promise.

# Resources

## Books

Glover, Beryl S. *Lost and Found–Recovering from a Loved One's Suicide*. 4953 Wythe Place, Wilmington, NC 28409. 1997. ISBN 0-943487-49-8.

Manning, Connie. *I Know Someone Who Died*. Oklahoma City: In-Sight Books, Inc. P. O. Box 42467, Oklahoma City, OK 73123, 800-658-9262, www.insightbooks.com. 1998. ISBN 1-892785-05-6.

Manning, Doug. *Don't Take My Grief Away From Me*. Oklahoma City: In-Sight Books, Inc. 1979. ISBN 1-892785-04-8.

————. *The Gift of Significance*. In-Sight Books, Inc. 1992. ISBN 1-892785-01-3.

————. *Lean on Me Gently–Helping the Grieving Child*. In-Sight Books, Inc. 1998. ISBN 1-892785-06-4.

————. *The Special Care Series*. In-Sight Books, Inc. 1993. ISBN 1-892785-02-1.

## Audio Tapes

Manning, Doug. " Don't Take My Grief Away From Me". In-Sight Books, Inc. ISBN 1-892785-15-3.

————. "Grief and the Holidays". In-Sight Books, Inc. ISBN 1-892785-17-x..

# Videos

Glover, Beryl S. and Glenda Stansbury. "The Shattered Dimension–The Journey of Life After Suicide". In-Sight Books, Inc. 1999. ISBN 1-892785-35-8.

Manning, Doug. "Grief in the Workplace". In-Sight Books, Inc. ISBN 1-892785-26-9.

**Beryl Glover**, from Wilmington, North Carolina, lost her daughter and brother to suicide in 1983 and her husband to a viral infection in 1993. She has participated in survivor support groups, facilitated meetings and presented at conferences and workshops. In addition to writing, she nourishes her soul in the company of family and friends, and by skippering her boat in search of dolphins along the Intracoastal Waterway.